Bright Side of Darkness

Flora L. Horn

authorHOUSE®

AuthorHouse™
1663 Liberty Drive
Bloomington, IN 47403
www.authorhouse.com
Phone: 1-800-839-8640

First published by AuthorHouse 2/11/2010

ISBN: 978-1-4490-7270-4 (sc)

Printed in the United States of America
Bloomington, Indiana

This book is printed on acid-free paper.

$\mathcal{I}$ am glad to be able to write this book and share it with my family and friends. It is very touching to go back and relive some of the heartfelt pain I have been through. As you read my book, you will understand why.

Going back in time and into time is just barely scratching the surface. Time is so precious, God gave it to me at birth and I gave it back to him. I gave him my heart and soul for keeps. He died for me, and I as I live and breathe it is because God has allowed me too. Even in all the darkness of dark, there was a shinning light. Had I not followed the light, I would always be stumbling in darkness.

I want to express to every reader there is always a Bright Side of Darkness. God is the Light of the world. I trusted this light at the age of thirteen and He accepted me as his child. Our minister's subject for that Sunday was Hands. I asked the Lord to come into my heart and used my hands for his service. He was our family minister; he had two children a boy and a girl. I was close friends with my minister's daughter and still friends to this day.

There have been many trials and temptations in these seventy nine years of mine, struggling to raise my children and provide for them was a big struggle. I can truly say without Gods help we could not have made it through all our sorrows and heart aches. We have had much joy too. I will get into the deep of raising my children.

I married at sixteen years old and had my first child in nine months. My husband joined the Air Force and was stationed a while in Black Land Air Force in Waco Texas. Soon after he was shipped over seas, I was alone to raise our child. I was now living with my mother-in-law and father-in-law to survive. Living in the country and we had no car and no way to get around. Relatives and friends would take us to the doctors if needed. We had our own little garden and a few chickens at that time. Survival depended on grit and determination. My in laws were of old age. My husband was their baby boy and he was born late in change of life and was very ill for a very long time. My mother-in-law spoiled our baby girl while we lived with them. She would give her cookies and coffee for breakfast. They became very attached to Leola. She was my love and I held her dearly to my heart. When she was two years old, I was in severe pain and could hardly walk. My sister lived several miles from us and I needed to get to the hospital. Our neighbor owned a dump truck and his wife owned a car. She was gone when I walked in, in pain to their house for help. He said this old truck is rough, but I will see you get to your sisters.

Arriving there, she asked what was wrong. I told her I must get to the doctors right away. Well my sister's husband was plowing in the filed a distance away. She went down the road to her in-laws and they agreed to help me. My sister packed a couple of gowns and off we went. Doubled over in pain and upon arrival in the emergency room the doctor asked me to step up and get on the table. When I did this, my pain quit. I said, "Doctor I do not understand". He examined me and said, you must have surgery right away, your ovary has rupture. I was so scared, no one to hold my hand.

My sister came as soon as she could get there. Her husband brought her and kept their children so she could be with me. Recovery took time.

News came, my husband was to go and leave for New Guinea. He took the German measles. Later was shipped out of the Philippines. I was lonely and weary, with pictures of him sitting around brought tears to my eyes. Leola, our little girl had learned to count to ten. She walked up to each picture and said, "I have one two three daddy's". We all chuckled.

While in the service he got his back slashed and cut into the muscle. Long suffering and healing he was finally released with a bad malaria fever. He was unable to work, and shaking with fever and chills. I had never experienced any thing like this before. He came home unable to provide for us.

Still living with his dad and mom we started looking for a place to live closer to town. He finally got a job driving a truck. That didn't last long as his back was tender from the wound. This malaria fever had kept him down too. This led me to seek a job to provide for us. I took a job as a waitress in a restaurant. I had to wait at a bus stop and ride to work. I had never worked in public at this time and I was a little nervous. It was quite different from working in the fields. I had to wear a uniform and hose. I was used to picking cotton and anything to do with filed work. My dad shared cropped when I was growing up. I had to quit school when I was thirteen and go with my dad and brothers to West Texas and bowl cotton, I had never seen cotton pulled before. Maybe you haven't either. After we picked cotton in the south, after a hard freeze dad and my brothers went to west Texas to bowl cotton. I was to cook for them and then go to the cotton patch (the filed). My brother's wife had taken the job, but got sever attacks of asthma and had to go home. She was with child and not able to continue working as a cook. I saw my first tumble weeds, sand storms, and first sections of land. No fences and never knew where the cotton row ended. It was quite an experience.

So you see my job as a waitress was different and much easier. No long white ducking sack hanging on my shoulders weighed down with cotton. I had to drag it or throw it upon my shoulder to carry out to the wagon to be weighed. Then my brothers would throw it up in the wagon empty it. Late in the evening I went to the tent and fixed their supper. Yes we lived in tents or what ever people had for us to live and work for them. I don't miss the cotton fields at all.

After working in the restaurant, we got a little money saved in time. We moved to Abilene Texas, where my mother and father worked from the fields. My husband got a job working in the Bairds Bread Bakery. All my brothers and in-laws had moved to west Texas for work. Two brothers and my husband worked in the bakery. Also my sister drove a Bairds Bread truck. I kept busy washing and taking in ironing, yes, white bakery uniforms and caps. I also started in nursing school at Hendrix Memorial Hospital in Abilene, Texas. I ironed in my spare time and waited on my father-in-law who became very ill. He would wander off, one day he went off on his own down the highway and had a car stop to pick him up and give him a ride. At that moment I saw what was going on and went to him, took him by the arm and said, "dad come on back to the house". They were living with us at the time. Finally we found a house that had a fenced in yard and they moved.

We still checked on them and took care as we could.

I finally got a job as a nurse aid at the Hendrix Memorial Hospital. I loved it. That was my calling to help people who were suffering. My little girl, (Leola) was six years old now and I was pregnant with my second child. I worked the three to eleven shift at the hospital and my mother cared for Leola until daddy got home from the bakery. My Mother and dad lived down the street from us about four houses from us. My sister also how Barbara got pregnant Velda lived across the street from us at the time.

Christmas holidays in the air and I was looking forward to seeing the city and the hospital decorated up with the beautiful lights and decorations. As a child we had very little to decorate with but we decorated with joy and laughter. Mother popped pop corn and we would string it on a string with a needle and thread. Then hang it on the tree in rope like. If we had some colored paper we cut that in small strips and glued on in a loop and continued to loop until we had a string of loops to hang on our Christmas tree. Mother made us always feel happy with what we had.

Christmas holidays were very tiresome as I was working night shifts at the hospital and pregnant at the time. I would get attached to some of my patients and families. A gentleman had bone cancer and he was in and out of the hospital. At this time he was nearing death. His lovely wife was much attached to me as I was assigned to his service. They had two lovely daughters, one was married and one was single. It was so tiresome for his wife to sit and watch him die. She seldom left the room. Christmas eve the married daughter asked her mother to go shopping a while and see the lights and decorations. They left the room, and about thirty minutes after they left he died. I had to console the daughter that stayed with him. He was covered up and we had to wait for his wife to return.

They returned and when she walked in the door she had two gifts in her hands. She started to cry and came to me and fell in my arms and handed me a gift, a doll, a pretty little girl. I felt so bad for her and her girls.

We hugged and then decisions were made and he was removed. I was called to another room to assist with a patient who was in a serious car wreck. His wife and little daughter came to the hospital to see him.

5

It was their daughters first Christmas. So needles to say not such a joyful Christmas spirit for many.

Being pregnant, I wasn't taking all this too well. Our little tree was well decorated at home and I was thankful I have my family to be with. I never had a glass doll or rubber doll when I was a little girl. Mother made little rag dolls for us. We made a dollhouse from a card board box. Cut windows out and pastes a rag over it for curtains. We loved our rag dolls. After Christmas we were on our way across town to see one of my sisters and there was ice on the streets. Before we arrived a man walked in front of us and my husband put his brakes on and we almost hit the man. I screamed and by then I could feel hot blood on the seat of my clothes. Our car stalled and my husband called from a store, for my sister to come and get me. I had a new princess green coat and it was soaked. I called my doctor and told him what had happened and he said if I had passed that much blood I must have miscarried. This was on Saturday and he said to come on in on Monday. I was alright and felt alright just felt weak. I never went to the doctor. I continued a monthly period after that so I thought I had lost my baby too. I kept gaining weight and still working at the hospital and soon I began to hurt. The doctor said to come in for a check up, and I was very much with child.

On July the twenty third I had a baby boy, Charles Edward Jr. after a few days I went home from the hospital. I resumed teaching my Sunday school classes. The first Sunday back to teaching my husband stayed home to care for the baby while I went to teach the class. When I got home my husband had the baby in his arms, he was walking and crying. I said, "What's wrong"? He said he quit breathing and couldn't almost get him to breathe. We got our baby to the doctor and he said he probably had a temper fit and held his breath. Our baby was about two weeks old, not old enough to have a temper fit as the doctor quoted. This happened often when he was laid on his back to be diapered he would stop breathing. So we explained this to the doctor and he wasn't concerned.

Much later my husband got real sick and almost died. He had taken the chicken pox. We were in a decision to move to Waco Texas and seek help with a pediatrician doctor that his sister had recommended.

In the mean time my mother kept Charles some as we made arrangements to move. When I went to get our little boy, my mother was crying and she said, "Flora he died, and then he came back alive"! He was still so pale he had the same look he had when it happened with his father. Mother was so shocked.

We left Abilene Texas and moved back to Waco, getting the baby help. The doctor said he would outgrow what ever it was. He said that when he was on his back the throat closed off some, and this was what was causing the fainting. He began to get better.

Two years after he was born I had another baby girl. She was another beautiful girl with blond hair and grey eyes. She was a doll to the other children. They wanted to hold her all the time. There was a six year difference between Leola and Charles Jr. and now two years difference between Charles Jr. and Barbara my new baby girl.

We had moved on a farm and were working in the fields again. Leola, Charles, and Barbara, who was one year old, had to go with us to the fields. My husband and I both had to work. He was sick a lot with horrible migraines headaches. He had a deep scar across the top or his scalp from a car accident when he was a young man. Sometimes

I had to take him to get injections to relive them pain. Times were so hard for us.

One day Leola asked if she could keep the children home as they were so tired sitting in the field by the wagon. The ants and heat were so bad. Our house was not too far from the field, so we agreed to let them stay home. Breakfast was cooked and there was lunch meat for sandwiches at noon. My husband and I went to work and up in midmorning Leola came screaming and running in the filed and we ran to her, and our baby girl (Barbara) had been burned badly on top of her head with hot grease. Charles wanted a fried egg, and Leola fried the egg. She had to step outside and use the out door toilet. When she stepped back into the back door she saw Charles was up in a chair shaking the skillet, the handle was loose. So when he picked the skillet up in cause the skillet to tip over and egg and hot grease fell on her soft spot on top o f her head and burned Barbara's scalp awful. I put Vaseline on the burn and she swelled up like a balloon. Rushing her to the pediatrician, he asked what I had put on it. Come to find out she was allergic to Vaseline. I then remembered when she was born and they placed her in my arms she looked like ants had stung her all over. The doctor said she was allergic to baby oil. I could not use baby oil on her at home.

Job changed for the better. My husband got a job with Austin Bridge co. and we had to move to San Antonio Texas. Barbara's scalp still healing, but she couldn't wear anything on her head. We settled in a tiny apartment and there was no heat in the bathroom. So we had a small heater plugged in when we took baths. Charles Jr. had his bath and climbed out and sat on the commode lid and slid off and his butt sat right on top of the heater. What's next I thought? But I never let

Satan get the best of me. Holding on to faith and praying for their healing I kept on going forward. Leola had grown in to a ten year old by now. I sewed my children's clothes. Her cousins lived in San Antonio and they visited together often. She was much more fortunate than we were wealth wise. She gave my daughter nice clothes but Leola wanted me to make her a dress to wear on a school trip to see the capital in Austin Texas; I made the dress for her.

While in San Antonio we visited the Alamo with the children after the burns healed and we visited the Chinese gardens.

Sometimes their dad had to work on weekends and we would go with him, and the kids would play in the dirt and watch him way up on the huge dragline. He would come home sometimes and say he had tied pig tail all day, I said, "what on earth is that"? He said, "It's where you twist some steel together". We had so many things we had seen and learned.

We had another daughter. She had a lot of red hair like me. We named her Carol Elaine. We had the name Elaine picked out and couldn't decide what other name to use. Her doctor's name was Doctor Carol. So we thought Carol went well with Elaine. Now we had three girls and one boy. Every time I went to the hospital Charles Jr. would say, "Mama asked the doctor to get me a brother". He was so sad when I came home with the little red headed girl. He cried and whimpered for days.

All went well and one night we were leaving his grandmothers house and it had been raining and was foggy to drive in. We heard the noise from the back seat and Leola thought the door was open some and she was going to shut it, well it flew open and she was hanging onto the handle. My husband slowed down and she fell to the street, about this time I jumped out of the car and ran to her, just in time as a car was almost going to hit her. We rushed her to the hospital to have her checked out. She appeared good and was released. I am sure most of you mothers have had your experiences too. I hope not all badly.

Continuing his job in the construction we moved a lot. While in Abilene, Leola turned thirteen years old. She was in Jr. High and a very beautiful child. We went to church everywhere we lived. My husband was ordained a Baptist Minister, but went to following construction work to provide for us.

One day Edward sr. came in tired and was getting ready for a shower when I went to my mothers house about six blocks from our home. Vacation bible school was to start the next day and my mother has a lot of flannel graphs of bible characters that she said I could use in the bible school. I had a skillet of potatoes frying, and told my daughter to stir them and I would be back shortly. As I left the house, with thoughts of getting my four children off to bible school the next day. I would have a day to rest for a short while.

When I got back, Leola was crying hysterically as she came in the back door. She said "mama I let the potatoes burn". I told her not to cry that I would fix some more. She seemed very frightened. I never had to spank her for any reason and I wondered why she was so upset.

Not knowing what really happened until we moved again to a little town called Troy Texas on a bridge job, did I find out the hard way of what had happened to her.

We lived just across from a little Baptist church. My husband, Leola and I sang specials at church together and sometimes he preached and went to jails for visits.

One day Leola had asked her father for some money to go to a ball game and he said he didn't have any money. She told him he had money for what ever he wanted but he we didn't have money for what we wanted.

A year later, after many trips to the doctors she broke down screaming, "I hate him, I hate him". I told her she must not hate any one. She said, "I do hate him, mother". She was sitting in the dinning table doing her school lesson, when she started hitting the table screaming. Her dad walked out and slammed the door. He knew she was going to tell me everything. She did.

She finally told me all the ugly details of the abuse, her dad had done to her.

It was the day I went to my mother's to pick up the bible school literature. She said he partly opened the bath room door and asked her to get the towel from the laundry room. She gave him the towel and he grabbed her by the arm and dragged her to the couch. She said, "He held her with great force and told her not to scream, I clawed him and kicked as hard as I could as he was forcing his fingers into me and I hurt so bad, I screamed as loud as I could". Her daddy told her not to tell me because I'd loose my baby.

I was pregnant with my fifth child. Leola kept her dark secret from me until my baby was born and she was nearly a year old when Leola broke down and told me everything. We struggled together through theses unbelievable tough and heart breaking times.

It is painful to talk about it. When she told me he tried to rape her a year before, that was the day she cried and said she let the potatoes burn. So many things came to my mind. Should I kill him? No the bible said, thou shall not kill. It did say I could leave him because of fornication.

When he came home I asked him why he did this to our daughter. He said he didn't know why. I said lets get a counselor or go talk to the pastor. It was no, no, no, no. So I told my family about all of this and he left us.

I was in great shock and cried so hard I couldn't see. My eyes were swollen and my hands were curled like claws. The muscles in my arms were as hard as a rock. Lora called the doctor and he ordered muscle relaxers for me and said, "Come to his office the next day". To think that my child had gone through all that abuses from her dad and kept it to herself shattered me.

I divorced my children's farther after twenty nine years of marriage, when I found out he tried to rape my oldest daughter, Leola. She kept it from me for a year. After this happened she became nervous at home and her grades were slaking off at school. She would come up with an answer like someone has stolen her gym shoes or one or her books was missing and she had to pay for it.

I told my family about all this and he left us. By now Beverly was just a little over a year old. I moved to Conroe Texas and applied for a job at the Conroe Hotel, when I went in for the interview the owner asked me where my home was. I said to him, "wherever I hang my hat and I don't have a hat". He said you do now. So I knew I had a job now. He said, "But, let me say this I will not fire my black kitchen help". I asked why he had made this comment. It seemed the help couldn't get along with her, but I didn't seem to have a problem with her. The waitress that had been there the longest was jealous of me.

I was hired and the first day I took an order, she didn't like the way I abbreviated the order and yelled out at me. I said, "Just tell me how you want it abbreviated". She couldn't, I spoke so calm. She liked me from the word go. We really hit it off. While working at the hotel restaurant the children and I lived alone. When I was at work a nice black lady I met and hired would sit down with my children and baby sit them. They enjoyed fishing together and they liked here very much.

One night the girls and my son, (Charles) were watching TV and Barbara screamed, "Mama someone is looking in our window". I went into the next room so I could see out and it was their dad. I called the police and they asked me to come to the police station and bring my children. So I did and we told them what he had done and he needed to be put away. They arranged a meeting between the judges and the doctors and him.

He said he didn't know why he did what he did. They told him to either volunteer to go to Rusk in Austin Texas or go to prison. He volunteered to go to Rusk. Rusk is a mental hospital in Texas.

Since he volunteered he could check himself out. He was informed of this by his boss. So he did, checked himself out with out after one month. I could not divorce him until he was out. Once he was out I did.

I worked a split shift to take care of my family. While I was working the night shift I was unaware of a young man coming over to the house to see my daughter Barbara. She had met him through a neighbor next door. Our neighbor was a young girl with a small child herself. One day Barbara asked me if she could a get a new bra and an A-line dress. Meanwhile I was noticing she was getting sick in the mornings. I had noticed that she wasn't having a menstrual cycle. I then put two and two together, is she pregnant? I couldn't believe that this could happen to my daughter. When I asked her if she was pregnant she turned very pale and said, "I guess I could be". So I made a doctors appointment for her and she was nearly four months pregnant. The doctor did blood work and the results came back and she was very anemic. She then had to have blood transfusions done. In the mean time I found out who this gentleman was and began my investigation. I found his name and parents information. So I made this telephone call to his parents and I came to find out he was married and had three children already. He and his wife were separated and they were in a different state. I let his parents of what he had been doing. I told them he had two choices, either go to jail or man up and pay all the medical bills. I confided in my brother as to what I should do. He said to come on home back to Texas. My brother paid our way back to Texas. So we left Arizona and moved back to Texas.

As soon as we got back we set up doctor appointments for her. During her pregnancy she would beg me to allow her to keep her baby. So as a mother my head was in a whirl wind on how I was going to manage with my children and this new baby my fourteen ear old daughter was expecting. Her baby boy was born on Thanksgiving Day in the Houston Hospital. I stayed with her until time for birth. The doctor came in and asked her to think about the name of the child and the legal right he would have if she gave him his last name. So the decision was made and he was named Eddie Helm, my daughter's name.

While working at the hotel restaurant I would call a taxi to take me to and fro from work. This gentle man introduced himself and gave me the number of his taxi, and when I would call I would request for him. If I would call and he wasn't there I would wait until he came on duty.

Thru this process we got to know each other very well. He was a good man very kind didn't drink or smoke. We talked about when he was in service and got closely acquainted. Before we got married he told me the lady he was married to before had five children and she wanted him to adopt them. They couldn't get along it was not a happy marriage. As soon as he signed the adoption papers she left him. He was stuck paying child support until the last child was turned eighteen. After a while we got married in the courthouse, by the justice of the peace. A few months into our marriage I became pregnant. This was a shock for the both of us, because as far as he knew he was infertile because he was never able to conceive a child.

I was now a mother of five lovely children, weary and worn from hard work and tough decisions. Struggling to raise my children alone with out any support from the children's father, I found myself pregnant with the children's step father.

Chester said he couldn't stand anymore responsibilities. He was angry that the children's father, Edward Sr. never contributed to the children's needs and I had to work to help my family. So he walked out.

Walking to work daily, I was tired by the time I got there. By the time I would get home from work I could hardly think. If I am lucky sometimes I get a ride home. The weight of my body and my tired feet, with swollen ankles was almost too much for me. Working as a waitress and carrying heavy trays, my doctor said I must stop working or I could loose my baby. Now! How am I going to provide food, shelter and medical bills for my children? Good question with no answer.

A nice couple I met at work came by to see me one day and they asked me how I was going to manage with all my obligations. My answer was, "I don't know"! Bill and Louise told me they would ask this friend of theirs if I could work her bar. They said Flora, you will serve beer. I will think about it very seriously. Knowing I had to have an income, I had to have a job, not much choice when you don't have a car to drive or a high school education. Both are essential in life.

Raising my children alone meant I had to arrange my work schedule, so the children that were in school would have care until I got home from work. My daughter, Barbara said, "Mother I will keep my sister while you work." Barbara is my fourteen year old daughter who had a very sick little baby. He cries day and night. She and I would get very little sleep. Hurting for her little one and my other children, the road of life looked dark. I remember the scripture my mother taught me, about how the Lord took care of the little birds and the lilies of the field. He will surely look after me and my little ones. My daughter Barbara took my hand and said, "Mom, I am sorry I got pregnant, which can't be helped now, but I want to thank you for not making me abort or give my baby up. So now I want to help you in any way I can."

My decision now was to change jobs. My friends came over one evening to let me know that Mrs. Cavell at the Horse Shoe Bar wanted to hire me. Bill and Sandy came to get me for my interview. I was more than grateful I didn't have to walk. Wearing a soft blue maternity dress and low heals of blue color, I felt confident and comfortable about myself. Mrs. Cavell introduced to me and smiled. She said, "I see you are going to be a proud mother before to many months." Bill and Sandy had already told May (Mrs. Cavell) my situation was rough. She was very happy to hear I was interested in working as long as I could. She couldn't seem to keep the young girls very long as they would meat a fast talker and take them and they would leave her stranded for help.

May, knew I would be steady help. But in my mind I had wondered if she would hire me, I was a few months of pregnancy.

She showed me around the bar and introduced me to some of her regular customers. They were nice and polite to me. She also said she had nice customers that would carry the beer out of the store room for you. They will pack the beer boxes for you too if you ask them to. May showed me the ropes per say and told me I could start to work the next day. There was a good feeling in my heart, knowing I had a job. Bill and Sandy bid May good day and said to her, "I bet she will be a good bartender". May then said, "She will do ok". Arriving home I thanked Bill and Sandy for taking me to meet May and for bringing me home.

My grandson, Eddie was crying and Barbara was worn out from walking the floor and rocking him. She was trying every thing to get him to stop crying. We had taken him to the doctor many times. The doctor couldn't find out why he cried day and night. Eddie had seizures and my concern for him was to find what was wrong with him, what causes these seizures.

My job is secure and I start to work tomorrow. The pantry is pretty bare. It is slim from pay day to pay day. Rent, utilities, school lunches, doctor visits and food. With the tips I made at the restaurant I had to pay a taxi to take my daughter and her baby to the doctor. The doctor told us the milk must not agree with Eddie or he could have chronic colic. He said, "If he doesn't get better he will send us to a specialist". In the mean time my neighbor, who was a mason said, "Flora, get that child to Texas Children Hospital in Houston Texas". The Masons will help you. The arrangements were made for my grandchild to enter the hospital within a week.

Again more decisions. Who will get to stay with the children until I get home from work exhausted? But the Lord will renew my strength. I have a job now to provide for my family. I will take this one day at a time. Supper over with and laundry folded, I will take little Eddie in my arms and rock him. He is still crying, so I walk him awhile and he eases off to sleep. Barbara and I take turns sleeping and carrying for Eddie. In pain a lot from being on my feet so long, I wonder just how long can I hold up to this job. Pushing and shoving thoughts aside, I pause and ask the Lord to help me endure what ever lies ahead of me.

Time has come for grandbaby Eddie's appointment at the Texas Children Hospital in Houston Texas. It is nearly fifty miles to this hospital. With no car I will have to get a cab to take my daughter and her baby there. I called my friend who drives one of the cabs here in town and asked the price of the fare to Houston"? She said, "For you the flat rate, zero", that is what my friends are for. She said Lora told me, "Flora, you are in much distress and I will help you in any way I can so call on me". Oh what a relief another burden lifted.

The phone rings and it is Sandy. She asked me if I was ready to tackle my new job. Head on I replied. I told her Barbara had to take the baby to the hospital and I would have to get a baby sitter so I could go to work. She told me she would take the girls home with her until Barbara got back. Bill and Sandy came and took me to work. I walked in the bar and was greeted by the boss and her costumers. The bar maid cleared the cash register for my shift. I was uneasy in a bar. I have never worked in a bar before and wondered if the costumers got out of line. People seem to go overboard with the bad language or sometimes insult you when they have too much to drink.

All went smooth my first evening. The costumers tipped well and seemed to like my service. The conversation came up about my pregnancy. One customer asked, why doesn't you husband support you? My reply was that it's personal. My work is my only income for support. He left a generous tip when he walked out. Facts are facts and I was about as low in spirit as I could get.

When Leola was seventeen she got married. She was afraid her husband would not love her if she told him what happened. Her father was taken to a doctor not by choice but by the law. I had reported him to the sheriff's office and they handled it from there. The children and I had to appear before a judge and tell our story. He was sent to a mental hospital and voluntarily admitted and didn't know why he did it. When he got out of the mental hospital his boss gave him his old job, we never saw him again. I filed for divorce and he never contested it. At the time of the divorce I had four children at home to provide for. Two were under school age. Years of continuous struggle and never enough money to make ends meet, I didn't think it could get worse. But it did.

Chester knew of a lawyer and went to talk to him about our situation. He told him that he didn't want to be responsible for this child. Once this lawyer was informed he knew of a family that wanted to adopt. The lawyer sent me a letter stating that I had to come into his office and see him. So I made an appointment and go talk to him. When I went to talk to him he told me I had to put up my child for adoption, or he would have my other children taken away from me. As he said I wouldn't be able to take care of them. My heart was so burden of this circumstance I found myself in.

Near time for the birth of my child, I had my lawyer call Chester so arrangements could be made and papers signed for some support to help with the medical bills. Chester said he didn't want any more responsibilities and he couldn't pay out any more money. He got mad, got a lawyer and filed for divorce. My heart was full of hurt, questions and worry. How can I support and care for Barbara and little Eddie and my other children at home?

The time came when I had to quit my waitress job as I was now in my seventh month of pregnancy with my sixth child.

One afternoon my friends, Bill and Sandy came to see me. They asked if I would consider putting my baby up for adoption and that they knew of a great couple that was looking. This was the same couple the lawyer knew of. This was deep blow to me. I said, "in no way would ever give my baby way"!

A few days went by and I told the lawyer about this family wanting to adopt my baby. He said, he would fix up all the papers and the medical bills would be paid by the family who would adopt the baby.

I called my brother very broken hearted and crying, he asked, "sis what is wrong"? I asked his advice about the difficult decision I had to make. He said, "Flora, if they are respectable people and have no children, they will be able to give your baby a good home". My brother Lewis told me that all my family would stand by me what ever decision I made.

The lawyer called the Johnsons and arrangements were made for them to meet and sign papers that they would pay all medical bills. The lawyer had me come in later to discuss the plans. He told me if I changed my mind after the baby was born I could keep him. This has been a heart breaking experience for me.

In labor, I was rushed to the hospital and taken to the third floor where my baby was delivered. I wanted another son when I had my other children. I had one son and four girls. Every time I went to the hospital and had a girl, my son, Charles would say, "Why didn't the hospital give me a little brother"? I told him they didn't have any little boys and he said, "Take the baby to another hospital and trade it for a boy". It was tough trying to explain to children the ways of life and why we have to do the things we do.

When the doctor came in the delivery room, he told the nurse to put me to sleep. Waking up I was out in a room with empty arms. My daughter Barbara came in and told me I had a pretty little boy with dark hair and they had boy H on his crib. I was shocked as I had told the family not to tell me. As I lay there in much pain, tears flowing, I said. "I want to call the lawyer; I don't want to give my baby up". My heart was racing with the unknown answers. Would I get to see my baby and keep him? The nurse came into my room and gave me a shot. As I was sedated she brought in a paper and told me to sign it. I said, "what for"? No answer. When I got the lawyer on the phone, he told me I couldn't keep the baby. I told the lawyer I wanted to see and hold my baby. He said if I changed my mind he would take all my children from me. By now I had drifted into a sleep from the medicine.

Awaking now, I learned the papers I had signed earlier were the final papers for the adoptive family to take my child home with them. The pain I had in my heart, no pain shot would ease it. Only time and prayers could bring healing in my mind and heart. The day I walked to the elevator was such an empty feeling in my stomach, knowing I had carried my baby close in me and now I couldn't hold him in my arms and take him home with me. I didn't know where he was going or who had adopted him tore my guts right out of me. Crying hysterically, my daughter Barbara said, "Mother some day he will grow up and I will help you find your baby, our brother". She wiped her tears with me.

Arriving home feeling lifeless, Barbara said, "Mother, Ernest and I are getting married tomorrow". Another shock! She and Ernest had been going to and fro to the hospital in Houston to see little Eddie. He was diagnosed as one of the thirteenth most critical children there in the children's ward.

Barbara had to learn how to give him shots in the front of his little legs. She had to put on her gown and her facemask before she entered the huge glass room where all the critical babies lay in their special cribs. The nurses and doctors had to give special care to these babies twenty four hours around the clock. Eddie was diagnosed with hypoglycemia (low blood sugar) and grandmal seizures. He was put on a special diet and was in the hospital most of his baby hood. Only getting to come home sometimes on the weekend after my daughter learned to give him shots.

It was back on forth to the hospital and home when Eddie did get to come home. Eddie has such a rare condition that would have to specially make his formula. It was a challenge when we would get low, since it had to be specially made. He continued to have seizures. Doctors had us to give him sweetened water or orange juice in his baby bottle. His sugar lever would get very low and he would go into a seizure or coma like condition.

Barbara and her husband started having trouble in their marriage. It didn't last long before they were divorce. Barbara had to work to take care or she and Ernest would step in to help with Eddie. They stayed good friends. Ernest got married to a lady who had two children. She

22

had a difficult time dealing with Eddies seizures. She did the best she could, all of us as a family would rotate taking care of Eddie. Who ever had Eddie at the time was responsible to take him to the Texas Children's Hospital for his appointments.

The two grandmothers Grandma Oliver and I would also take Eddie to church.

The only job Barbara could get at the time was working in a hospital cafeteria because she wasn't an adult yet, she was so young.

Some times we could bring Eddie home on the weekends from the hospital. During these times I would spend with him we would look at the photo albums, witch he enjoyed so much to look thru. He also loved to get into my button box and play with them; he was fascinated with threading them. He could spend some time playing with them and keeping himself entertained. Eddie loved too go out and eat, because he didn't get to do that with the Oliver's.

When Eddie started to go to school it was difficult on him. He would go in a seizure and the other children would be afraid of him. Some of the children made fun of him. Weekly he had doctors' appointments for a long time, then monthly. Then it was every other month. As he got older they thought he would out grow the seizures, but he never did. Eddie had a very difficult time in his teens, falling with the seizures and not being able to drive. Some of his friends were ashamed to take him out with them, afraid he'd have a seizure. When he was twenty one, I told the doctors there had to be a medicine to control his seizures. So he went to go see a specialist.

At age twenty seven my grandson was diagnosed with cancer.

This was another dark side of life, of all of us.

While Eddie was very critical in the MD Anderson Cancer Hospital we rallied in and out of the hospital with him.

During this time his mother Barbara, began looking for her brother. She went to the court house and looked up records with help and learned Boy H had a name. She learned his address and even drove near the house, but did not try to contact him until she called his parents. When Barbara called, Mr. Johnston answered the phone. Barbara said, "I am looking for my brother that was adopted by you and your wife". He paused and then called out to his son. "Do you still want to meet your real family?"

Rodney said, "Oh yes dad". Barbara and Rodney talked at length and she said, "Mother he asked about you and when could we all get together and meet"? She told him to meet in her home the next day and we would all be there.

That night I got a phone call from Barbara and asked me if I would have a coffee pot on? And I said, "No but I can make some". Brewing the coffee cars began to drive up in the driveway. I thought what was going on? Three of my four girls and their husbands drove in about ten pm. This was the mysterious, and I thought what is the meaning of all this? As they walked up the steps, the men stayed on the front porch and told the girls to bring their coffee out there. I poured all of us some coffee and I was the last to the table. Barbara and the girls talked a few minutes and they made sure I was sitting down. Barbara looked at me and said, "Mother, we have something to tell you". My heart went weak. I burst into tears, "don't tell me Eddie is gong to die"?

All the girls came and put their arms around me and I really panicked. All at once the said, "No mother, it is good news for a change". Wiping my tears and blowing my nose. I said, "It is about time for some good news".

"The good news mother is we found your son"!

Hysterically I said, "When can I see him"?

Barbara said, "Mother he asked the same thing". He was so anxious to see and meet us. This Saturday evening before the girls came to tell me they had found him; Barbara made all the arrangements to meet at her home the next day on Sunday evening at one pm.

Of course my son was overjoyed and so were we and it was hard for Barbara to tell him to wait until Sunday. She still had to tell her youngest sister, Beverly. This way we, as a family would see him together as a family.

I thought it was extra special of Barbara to arrange it that way. She said, "Mother it would not have been fair if I had met him without all of us.

I will say from Saturday night to Sunday evening seemed like another eternity. Too excited to sleep, I wept with joy and praised the Lord for answering my prayers of many over the years. Wondering what my son looked like and would he accept us as his family. Barbara had told me he asked what his mother was like and she told him I was a feisty thing and out worked them. I was happy to know there was no more Baby H. my son had a name and two families. We learned that the couple, who has adopted him, also had adopted a little girl. We learned my son was about to be a father.

He too had lots to tell us. So you can see and feel the excitement we were going through waiting. Making it through the night was tough. I counted the sheep and morning came with anticipation. Arising early I went to the store and bought doughnuts to take over to my daughters for us to munch on with our coffee. Although it was not one pm yet, my other girls and their families began arriving at different times. We began lunch plans. The men got the horse shoes ready to play in the back yard later in the evening.

Barbara's husband got the camcorder ready for action. My grandson, Eddie was very sick with his cancer but he was waiting to meet his uncle who was just a year younger than he.

A white truck drove in the drive way and a tall young man got out and walking towards the front door. Barbara was watching out the window for him to arrive. She said, "That must be him". The girls flew out the door to meet him. My four girls hugged and kissed him and they looked around and said. "Mother aren't' you coming"? I said, "I want to be last so I can hug his as long as I want to".

Rodney and I embraced with tears of joy, lingering in each others arms. Oh what a feeling to hold my baby for the first time.

The hot July sun bearing down on us, Barbara said, "Let's go in where it's cool". Son had a cowboy hat and boots and was wearing tight blue jeans. Tall like his youngest sister. He wore a small reddish mustache over his bright smile. What a bright light in the sight of my eyes.

We sat on the couch, me on one side of him and Barbara on the other side. His other sisters sat on the floor with their arms on his lap. It looked as if he would smother. It was a great reunion "The Bright Side of Darkness".

I think the darkest day in my life was when I walked out of the Montgomery County Hospital in Conroe, Texas without my baby in my arms.

Now almost twenty seven years later I get to hold him. We each had so many questions for him and, he had some for us. He said,

"I often wondered what my real family was like". He had asked his adopted dad how many sister or brothers did he have. His adoptive dad told him he really didn't know but several and I wasn't able to care for all of them and I had adopted him to them. He told his adoptive dad he wanted to find us.

He said, "I wonder if my real family would accept me" and he wiped his tears and hugged me. I told my son we had never forgotten him and prayed we would find him before I died. I explained all the hardship I went through. He understood.

I said to him, "See that young man across the room in the rocker? That is Barbara's son, Eddie". She gave birth to him at age fourteen and he was a very sick child and had to be hospitalized most of his life. When Eddie was little I was pregnant with you. He and Eddie became very close. Rodney told us he had been living within thirty miles of us all these years and yet we had never met. We had years of catching up. No way could we do it in one afternoon.

As the day passed on, his adoptive dad called Barbara's home to see if Rodney was ok. He asked him if his family was what he expected. Rodney told him yes and much more. He said, "Well I just wanted to know if you were enjoying yourself".

Rodney told us his adoptive dad asked him if he would like him to come along with him to meet us and he told his adoptive dad no, that he wanted to be alone with us.

He even left his pregnant wife home alone to come be with his family alone.

Lunch was spread on the table, help yourself style. With the camcorder still rolling, everyone was enjoying our first reunion together with Rodney. We all brought our special dishes of food to share. He ate like a pig and bragged about our cooking. His wife being pregnant didn't cook too often.

After our late lunch the men went outside in the back yard and teamed up for a game of horse shoes. Eddie and Rodney were partners. My son-in-law Brent, another son-in-law were partners. I couldn't seem to get Rodney out of my sight. I followed them outside and watched them play. Barbara took over the filming as her husband pitched horse shoes. They popped a few beers later after the game. The evening was going too fast.

Back in the living room relaxing and talking as we would never catch up we began to make plans for our next meeting.

Darkness came and Rodney said, "I wish we could just throw down sleeping bags and spend the night talking", but he had to go home. It was hard to see him leave but I knew our family circle was longer broken.

Bidding Rodney good night with contentment in our heart, as we haven't had since his birth. The next week Rodney called Barbara and Carol and they made dinner date to meet his adopted parents. The Johnston, they were pleased that Rodney had found his real Mother and sisters. Rodney had a brother he hadn't met at that time of this writing.

After lunch with his folks, they made plans to have a big Bar-b-Q at their place. There was lots of excitement in the air for everyone. The Bar-b-Q get together for Rodney's two families was a great turn out. We met my son's wife and step son, his adopted parents and many friends and relatives on both sides of the family. We filmed with the camcorder every thing for future memories.

Again the men gathered to choose partners to pitch horse shoes. After lunch plans for his first birthday were made even though he was grown. Barbara has been taking the bull by the horns per say. Rodney' adopted parents accepted us as if they had known us always. His in-laws were there, many, many friends anxious to meet us and get to know who we were and what we were like. It was beautiful reunion to remember. July passed so fast.

August the twenty fifth is Rodney twenty seven Birthday. The girls and I are making plans for his birth party. And I am so grateful Barbara has. She has handled every thing so graciously.

Barbara made reservations ahead of time at the Western steak house. She then contacted the lady whose name I can not recall who took care of all the adoptive papers and located Rodney for us and invited her presence at Rodney's birthday party as she played the vital role in us finding my son.

I invited my niece to come and bring her camcorder and film the party for us. This was a surprise party. Barbara called Rodney on his cell phone and asked him to meet her for lunch at the steak house and he said he would. The day of another celebration was coming up.

August 25, 1993

*T*he girls and I arrived early at the steak house to decorate the little room we reserved for this special occasion. We placed our gifts on one table and hung the birthday balloon on the back of his chair. We arranged it to where he would be sitting at the head of the table. The lady from the court house that told my daughter how to find him sat to the left of Rodney and I sat on the right when he arrived for lunch. Barbara met him at the entrance and brought him back to where we were. We burst our, "happy Birthday"!

He was so shocked, but happy. We had bought a dozen of red roses for our miracle lady as a token of our appreciation for helping us find my son.

Rodney came direct from work to lunch. As he walked in, my niece started filming my son's first birthday party. That is our first with him.

Barbara introduced the special lady to Rodney and she told him she had gone to school with his dad.

She had to make her visit short and get back to work at the court house. She thanked us for her roses and lunch and left the party for us to enjoy with Rodney.

He opened his gifts from each of us, with excitement. "Hey", he said, "a set of horse shoes". He went on and on, gasping as he opened his presents.

He came to my gift it was a wrist watch to hang on the wall. This was a very large time piece. I said to him, "this is a very special time for a very special person and all the times I thought of you. Time has brought you back to me in Gods time. Remember time is on our side". He had many gifts and cards. He said he would read his cards at home.

His sisters and I stood behind him and pictures taken. We had more beautiful moments to come.

Rodney and Eddie became close buddies. They spent a lot of time together. Rodney knew I gave him up to help raise Eddie and his fourteen year old mom, my daughter and Rodney's sister.

Rodney took Eddie home with him often. He and his other family owned and operated a big nursery and landscaping business. They had a large deer lease. He would take Eddie with him to the lease when Eddie was able to go.

Getting weaker and spending a lot of time now at MD. Anderson Cancer Hospital, we did everything we could to make Eddie happy. He loved to hunt, but with him having seizures, he was not allowed to go alone.

Rodney had asked Eddie what he wanted for his birthday. He said, "I want to go deer hunting and kill a deer". So Rodney went to Barbara's and picked Eddie up and to the deer lease they went on November twenty four. Rodney said he no more than got in the deer stand, he heard a shot and Eddie had killed an eight point buck. Eddies wish had been granted. He never knew that a party had been planned for later that evening at the deer camp. Friends and relatives knew Eddies' life was short and we wanted to fill it with as much happiness as we could.

Getting up so early and he tires so quickly he was ready to lie down.

Rodney hung the deer up and had Eddie stand by it and take a picture on the camcorder. Late evening the smell of Bar-b-Q and music playing, we arrived at the camp. Eddie asked, "What's going on"? I said, "No telling, you know they always have some kind of activity going on out there".

As he got out of the car, shouts of Happy Birthday rang out. He could hardly stand up he was so weak. There were many gifts and lots of food. There were decorations of balloons and the camcorder rolling.

Everyone settling down to eat, Eddie's cake was brought out and the magic candles wouldn't blow out. He tried to blow out his candles and finally he told his mother to blow them out. When she couldn't blow them out he laughed and said, "You knew I couldn't blow that kind out". To see how Rodney catered to Eddie was amazing.

Finding Rodney the later part of July we had our first birthday with him August the twenty fourth, reunions, Eddies birthday celebrated we pressed on. The days were full of joy and, being able to share life with my long lost son. To have a place in our life as Eddie's life was being shorten. It seems to me the Lord gave me back my son as I had given him up to care for Eddie when he was born to my fourteen year old daughter.

Eddie and Rodney have played a very special part in our lives. Oh how I love them. All my children and grandchildren and great-grandchildren are very special to grandma Flo.

As you have read and continue to read, you can see why.

November behind us now, December coming on, I was looking forward to having my first Christmas with Rodney, that turned twenty seven in august. It is like one big world circulating in happy holidays. Yes and it is for this mother who waited and prayed for nearly twenty seven years to find her son that was adopted out. I never gave up looking for him or gave up hope. I knew some day I would find him.

There is no book big enough to hold all the joy and experience we have shared together through my life.

I am now seventy five years old. And I am going to laugh, and I am going to live and I am going to love just for today and every day until my departure from this planet.

December 1993

*J*oy to the world, our family circle is completed now with Rodney in our life. We all come and go in our own ways and celebrations.

This is our first Christmas with Rodney. What a feeling of praise and joy at this special Christmas. I can feel the joy mother Mary had when baby Jesus was born, and then the years to come she had to give him up on the cross. But he arose, halleluiah and he is our heavenly Father.

He answered my prayers and renewed my life by giving me back my son. Rodney was my Christmas gift. This was the greatest gift of all.

Shinny wrapping on all the gifts under our tree, cannot out shine the glow of happiness I feel. My family glows with me.

Rodney shared special time with us and then went to his parents home to celebrate with his other family and friends.

January 1994

*M*any good times with our families and sad ones, but we can face them together. Good news, Rodney has a little girl and she is the youngest granddaughter and very special. She has proud parents and grandparents.

Time passes by too fast and I want to keep time with my family as long as I can.

Eddie is getting weaker. He is in and out of the hospital often, taking chemotherapy, blood transfusions, or platelets and much more.

As you read we take the bad with the good and press on. I didn't say it was easy.

I could go on with my family history in lengths. I will not leave you hanging out the window so to speak.

The bright side of darkness came when I found my son and got to see him for the first time.

Darkness has come many times but different lights shine in my darkness. One shinning light is Baby Kacee; my granddaughter was born with liver cancer and had surgery at two months of age, and was in the hospital for a year. She is in full recovery now and nine years old.

My grandson Eddie was admitted in the cancer hospital and his life was up. The day baby Kacee was released from the hospital was the same day Eddie was admitted. Eddie as you read is critical.

June 1995

*E*ddies cancer doctor has told us the chemotherapy and blood transfusions are not helping Eddie. My daughter and I are devastated. Eddie said, "Dr. Hill, if it's not doing me any good why do I have to keep coming to and fro for blood"? The doctor said, "Son you don't have to". Eddie said, "Then I and not coming back". Dr. said, "It is ok Eddie".

My daughter asked the Doctor, how long did my grandson have? The answer came while I was in Abilene, Texas for our fortieth family Foller reunion. With one week or less I

Rushed home, I went right to my grandson bed side and by my daughter side. He was alert up to his death. He gripped my hand at six am. And said, "Grandma"! I said, "I'm here for you honey it's ok to let go". He did.

The bright side of darkness is he is in his heavenly home free from cancer and heartaches.

God had placed Rodney back in our lives before he took Eddie.

We go with out lives the best we can.

My oldest daughter Leola, the one whose father had abused was in bad health for several years. She was able to attend Eddie's funeral in a wheel chair with oxygen.

Time was going fast for her too.

Rodney has been faithful through thick and thin. His heart was broken when Eddie passed. He had played a huge part in Eddie's and our lives since we were together. He was close to his sister's side before Eddie died.

Rodney was heart broken as he could see so much illness in the family and he has just really got to know us. He would come to see Leola and push her in the wheel chair out side for a while.

The time came, the last year of her life. I was helping my daughter, Carol, who cared for her full time. She would come in the morning and stay until about one pm. I came and stayed most all the time until morning. Sitting with her and giving her medications.

When I had to change her diapers, she would look into my eyes and say, "mama you changed my diapers when I was a baby and you should not heave to change them now". I told her, "It is ok dear someone may have to do it for me someday". She wiped her tears and squeezed my hand.

The bright side of darkness, Baby Kacee now, was going to school and would come over and hold my daughters hand and visit with her before she went to school. She would do this every morning while she waited for her school bus to come by and pick her up. She liked that and we all called Baby Kacee our miracle baby. She was a very bright side of darkness for sure.

So even with darkness we had a bright side of darkness.

Everyone of our family was coping well with darkness. We have seen the bright side and look on the bright side of darkness.

1998

*H*ospice came and went to my daughter's home she passed away August the twentieth of nineteen ninety eight, five days before Rodney was thirty two years old.

Again, Rodney was by our side as a family.

She went peacefully. No more struggling for breath. There is sunshine after the rain. And the sky doesn't stay dark all the time.

Now another side of darkness, is the reason Rodney hasn't met his brother is because he went to prison just before we found Rodney. This is why I cried out, "it is about time to hear some good news".

When I learned that my son, Charles was in prison, I cried my heart out. He had been in jail for six months before I knew any thing was wrong. I had sold my home and he did not know my address. Neither did I know his.

One night his son and ex-wife went by one of my daughters and told them where my son was.

I had to go to the doctor with my nerves. It was such a shock. This was all taking place in the later part on July nearing my son Charles birthday. My grandson was lingering in and out with cancer, and the joyful news of finding my other son, too much at one time.

I must write to my son, but what do I say? I can't say, "Happy birthday", as I couldn't be, so I thought.

So I cried out to God, "This is 911 God you have to help me". "What can I write"? The answer came, "tell him you love him". With tears flowing on my paper I thanked Jesus for the answer. I began to tell him I loved him and missed him. Of course a few questions a mother wanted to know. For sure he didn't need a lecture, only assurance he was loved.

He accepted Christ through faith and prison ministries. He has served as a chaplain's secretary and song leader in the prison ministry. He met a nice lady in church service, who came from the outside services to sing and play the piano.

Charles took seminary courses and served God faithfully, he and Kay became very close in a godly relationship.

Now time is being served with a bright side of darkness.

They became very good friends in Christ and after a period of assurance they got married by the chaplain in the prison. She loved him beyond a shadow of doubt.

I drove 400 miles to attend my sons wedding. The wedding was plain and simple, but with strong love, bound by God. No flowers and no cake. He wore his prison uniform that was white, she wore a white dress and her youngest daughter did too. It might have been a thirty minute visit among us.

This is another bright side of darkness. He is happy in the Lord and happy in marriage. He is coming home august this 2001.

I am grateful I can see the bright side of darkness.

Since all of this has happened in the past my age now has reached eighty three years old.

Now that Eddie has past away, his nephew Andy still celebrates his birthday with memories of Eddie. Their birthday was on the same date but different ages. His mother Carol would always make them matching birthday cakes. The last one that I remember before Eddie past away was a set of football helmet with the Cowboys football logo.

Since I was very close to my grandson, I kept him deeply in my thoughts. One night after eight years of his death, I was awakened by his voice and appearance in my bedroom doorway. He said, "Grandma

I'm home". It was clear and loud enough to recognize him in my doorway. I rose up in my bed and his appearance disappeared. He let me know he was home safe witch is now his heavenly home. It was his way of letting me know not to worry about him anymore. He was now free of seizures and cancer.

After my daughters and grandsons death many things came to happen. A friend of mine from Florida called one day and asked me if I could come and help her take care of her brother. He had had a major stroke and required a lot of assistance. I prayed about this for some time and made my decision final. I was now moving to Florida. I then started the moving process. I gave and sold some of my furniture and belongings. Almost everything I owned, except for the things that I could fit in my car and take with me. I had my four sisters come to my home before I did any of this. I had them go thru the apartment and pick things they wanted to keep and gave it to them. In my home I had two beautiful white doves that sat on my table and I gave them to my friend a thirteen year old girl, who had spinabipheda. She would come over to my apartment in her wheel chair. She loved to play with my doves. When she found out I was moving she asked me what I was going to do with the doves. I knew she would love to have them, so I gave them to her. Through this process there was a bright side to all of this. I had met another child with the same medical condition as my thirteen year old friend. I knew that I needed to bring these two together. I had asked their mothers if we could get them together so they could meet and they agreed. So their mothers brought them over in the wheel chairs and the two of them came to my apartment and met. The day they came over was Halloween so we made popcorn balls and the two girls placed the popcorn balls in Ziploc bags and sat at the entrance of our apartment and gave children popcorn balls for Halloween. The two girls turned out to be good friends. The bright side of this story about the girls is Faith who was thirteen at the time and whom I'd know since she was very small had made a new friend. Her new friend I introduced her too, passed away that December. Faith now works at Wal-Mart in the clothing department, giving people their room to try on their clothing, in Conroe Texas and is twenty five years old. She works from her wheelchair and get along just fine. As my readers read this book I want them to know there is always a bright side from darkness.

The day of November the twenty fourth, Barbara came to the apartment. She was on her way to put flowers on Eddie's grave. It was eddies birthday. She brought me a coffee thermos, instant coffee, and the local news paper. She also brought me stationary since my children know I love to write and keep in touch with everyone. There were a lot of hugs exchanged before I would leave. She stayed right with me until I loaded everything in my car that was coming with me to Florida. Barbara turned the key to the apartment and locked the door for me. She then turned the key into the office for me and that was that. This was starting a new chapter in my life and leaving some of the good and bad behind. This reminded me of some of Gods words from the bible.

My bible was my road map on this trip. It was in the front seat with me. God leads me, and his word says he will never leave me or forsake me. My friends, church, and organizations were sad to say goodbye to and sad to see me leave. Barbara asked me to stop when ever I felt sleepy or tired no matter how many hours I had driven. So I made an overnight stop in a little motel along the roadside. Once I was able to get my room and settled in I made phone calls to let everyone know

I was ok and that I would call them all once I made it to Florida the next evening. The next morning I was up early having my coffee in the motel and I was on my way. I followed all the directions on the map that was given to me. Arriving near my destination I called my friend on the cell phone and asked where to meet her. As I had never driven to Florida. I had been once before but had flown in to a poetry convention back in 1986. I was told just to stay on US1 until I got to Cheney Hwy. and she would meet me at the Best Western motel. I got to Florida in the late evening, tired and weary, not knowing where I was going. I pulled into the motel and went inside and called my friend and told here I was their and she then came and met me. I spent the night at her home for it was too late to get things started at the place I would be staying at. Early in the morning she showed me where her brother lived. This was the brother I was to take care of from the stroke he had suffered. He had his own condo where he lived. She gave me the key to the condo and called her son to help me unload all my belongings from my car. The condo was located on the second floor so we had to walk upstairs. There I was in a strange condo, all alone. I was told a shuttle was to go up that night at the Kennedy Space Center. I did not know what to expect. And was warned not to be alarmed from all the commotions and sound the shuttle would make as it took off. The condo was right across the river that faced the Kennedy Space Center. I got my belongings put away in my closet. And waited for the big boom to go off, I knew I wouldn't be able to sleep until that happened. Sitting on the patio facing the river, I watched the shuttle take off and after the boom I was ready to go to bed. I called my children and let them know I had made it in safe. They were so glad to hear from me and excited that I had the opportunity to see the shuttle launch. The patient that I had come to take care of was still in Sea pine Rehab Center. So when morning came I had the directions to the rehab center and to check with them what my duties would be when they sent him home. When I had the chance to see him He was still speaking with a slur, and cried a lot. So they told me I would have to work with him on his speech. They gave me a list of words that I would have to have him repeat after me. I was also told to walk with him daily. His sister would come over and have a walk with us also. He returned back to health and was able to go back and work as a sales person at Willow Lakes Estate.

I then moved into a living facility and took care of stroke patience. Five people lived in this house that I had to take care of. Some of them were stroke patience and some fighting with cancer. I was the only employee taking care of all five of these patience. The manager came as she pleased and didn't help with anything. I was solely responsible for all of them. My day with them started at 6am with meds, after that it was time to prepare breakfast for them. Right after breakfast I started the daily chores first one was laundry, while laundry was on I worked on the lunch menu, in between all of this I would also have to take care of their individual needs. Such as clothing, bathing, and small things like brush their hair. After lunch was naps, while they slept I did all the floors, sweeping and moping them all. Then it was time for dinner and meds and my day ended at 11pm after all their medications where distributed. I had to be presentable at all time incase of any type of emergency. I was on a twenty four hour call. After a few months of this I was overworked. One morning when I got up I blacked out. When I came to I managed to get myself to the bathroom and wash my face. I called the manger and gave my resignation; I knew my body couldn't handle any more.

After leaving this job I was told by a friend of a group of sisters that were looking for help. So I went over to their house and met everyone I was to be working with. I was satisfied with my work and they were satisfied with mine. This was a five day straight job, and on Saturdays and Sundays I would go and work with another elderly couple that was confined to their hospital beds. I worked from eight am to eight pm.

When I worked for these sisters I was expected to cook meals, do laundry, and take them to their doctor appointments. I worked for many years with them, and became very close to each and everyone of them. To make thing easier on them and on me, Mrs. Covell's son insisted I move in their little cottage in their back yard. It was a one bedroom cottage. Kitchen and bathroom a very quaint little place just for me. On the bright side of this, two nice ladies and their husband invited me to their house for Christmas.

I was Chaplin of the ladies auxiliary and visited the veterans and families. Every morning I would go by the VFW and have my first cup of coffee and read the bulletin board and get updates on who was ill and who was in the hospital. It was my duty to visit and keep things up to date. While on one of my visits I was asked to visit this veteran, witch I did.

One day I walk into a veteran's room to visit. When I walked into his hospital room a nurse was by his bed side giving him an IV. I had not met this member personally before this day. As soon as the nurse left the room I walked over and introduced myself to him as Chaplin of the ladies auxiliary, we chatted for a short while and I asked him before I left if he would mind a word of prayer. He said sure, so I held his hand and said a prayer. On this day I visited two other ladies from the auxiliary while I was there. The next day when I went to make my visits he was not there. I didn't see him for several days. I walked in one morning to the VFW to have my usual coffee and the veteran I ha met at the hospital was sitting on the opposite side of me. He was at the bar where I was having my coffee. So I said to him, "I went back to visit you and you had disappeared into the sunset". He said, "right after your visit in the hospital they medivac me to the Florida Hospital to have two stent put in my heart". He said he was doing well. I was told when I was coming in the VFW, that he had been asking for me and wanted to know who I was. He was informed that I was a widow and he was one himself. After a short time period, he got the courage to come and talk to me. He then thanked me for visiting him in the hospital. Out of the blue he asked me if he could take me out to dinner some time. I said, "That would be a nice treat". After our nice dinner he found out I loved to dance, and he was a swell dancer. Weeks past by and I invited him to my cottage, it was one way in and one way out. He asked me how I could live there. He said I was on a dead end street one door in and same door out. During his short visit he said, "I have a three bedroom home, you are welcome to have two rooms and a private bathroom and share the living room and kitchen". So he helped me move into his home. I took the one bedroom for my office so I could read and write my poetry and books in private.

The next invitation was valentine dance. We had a wonderful night along with our friends. He had flowers ordered and put out on our table that he had reserved. The flowers came with a little tiny bear, with flower pedals around his neck. When you would squeeze its hands it would say, "Love me love me not".

Leaving the little cottage was not an easy to do. I had to find a future for myself. I took a twelve months course with Long Ridge

Writers to get my writers certificate. After attending these courses I was told by the instructors that my works was so good it was ready to be published. I've been writing for many years, I have material packed in briefcases, drawers and files. That no one has ever read. I hope to surprise my readers some day with my work and talent. I have a variety of works from poetry, short stories and books.

My friend whom I moved in with owned an RV. The RV had been parked at his sons' home and had been sitting there for two years. One day he took me to see the RV and I was glad that he was going to move it closer so we could travel in it. Some friends of ours insisted that we join the good Sam's club. This I a club of people with RV's that do traveling together in groups. We joined the club. We did this for a few months and we enjoyed our trips and experiences with other people. At this time I was still able to read and write and would put some of my experiences on paper. We traveled the open road for about four months. During these months we visited many parks here in the state of Florida. The experience I had at Beverly Beach was a very memorable one. We had our RV facing the beach and there was a deck that you could step onto and look out into the water. At the time we had our little dog Blue with us. We would take him out for walks and let him take care of his business. We could see in the distance couples that would walk along the beach. The sand on the beach was wet enough that it would leave foot prints behind them. This sight reminded me of the poem "footprints" the one about Jesus carrying us in his arms and being only able to see one set of footprints that were his. Each night we had bingo in the club house, different people would make meals and we enjoyed sharing the time together and having fellowship. We also had auctions from time to time. And during the holidays we would take can goods to those who needed them and were less fortunate that us. So many in our RV group have now passed away. As I have no personal family in Florida, I claim my church family and my personal friends that are neighbors. I have been blessed in so many ways. So many were not able to traveling any more and Gene lost interest and sold his RV. He said he didn't feel safe driving the RV anymore. He said he thinks his age was catching up with his body. Driving such a bi vehicle is tricky.

Later on he bought himself a new car. We would travel to Pennsylvania his home place where he was raised. The history of his home place was very interesting to me. He told me his niece now owned the home he was raised in and is still in the family till this day. We toured the town the old groundhog place. We had an opportunity to visit the ground hog while we were there too. He showed me the old black smith shop where he helped his dad while growing up. The only school friend we visited was his friend Spud whom he was childhood friends with. We enjoyed our visit with his niece and his best friend. His best friend gave me a home made rocker made by the ommish people. It was so nice of him to do this for me. Gene had it shipped out to our home, it was too big to travel with and fit in the car. It has a perfect spot in the lanai. We enjoyed a quiet moment sitting in the old rocker.

After we left Pennsylvania we visited his sister in New Jersey. While we were there we visited many garage sales. I enjoyed all of this, so much to see and so many different things to enjoy. We helped her clean her flower beds and do things around the house. We had a great time visiting her, for this was the first time that I had met her. She is a very special person to know. After a few days, it was time to continue our road trip. We drove to visit his other sister that lives in Delaware. We had a great time with her and her son in their home. She called her daughter and husband and they all took us out to an evening meal. We drove over a Chessa Pete Bay to get to her home and it was an amazing bridge we had to cross over it. While we were there she taught us how to play monopoly for we had never played it before. She shared her family picture albums with us and got to know some of her side of the family. We really enjoyed the time with her. We continued on our journey and also made a stop in North Dakota and visited Gene's daughter. In North Dakota his daughter took us out in her car as she knew how much driving we had done. She took us to Mount Rushmore to see the carved faces of some of our presidents. She took us thru the Black Hills, a national animal park, and on the way back home she took us to an area in North Dakota where a lot of home made things are sold. This was nearing the end of the day so on the way home she stopped at a nice restaurant for dinner. While we were there we had the opportunity to ride a tourist train up and down the hills side of North Dakota. What a beautiful view. The first time I had met his daughter she had flown to Texas to meet us, so this was not our first time meeting each other. We spent a whole week with her enjoying all these activities.

We then left North Dakota and headed to Colorado. I had always wanted to visit all these states, since I had never had the chance or opportunity to visit these wonderful places. As we drove thru we spent the night in Colorado and left early in the morning and drove to Texas. We spent some time with my family in Conroe Texas. We took a couple of days rest before heading back on the road to travel back to Florida. At this time my eye sight was still good. So I would write at night about my experiences and visits. On this trip I wrote full book.

When we got back home, I had to get neck surgery. I had been suffering from neck pain for many many years. I suffered from degenerative disk in my neck. I had the best neck surgeon in Florida Dr. Deukmejian. Some people might see this as a dark side but I saw it as a bright side. The surgery was to repair my 4th 5th 6th and 7th disk, they put in a metal plate and screws to alleviate the pressure, and it was a successful surgery. I had to wear a neck brace for support for some time for healing to take place. But after it was all said and done, I came out feeling great. I was so thankful for being pain free. I would recommend this doctor to anyone anywhere.

I have been going to the First Christian Church since 1998 and at different times they have mission trips to the Bahamas and Haiti. The year of 2005 the church had a mission trip to the Bahamas planed and I signed up for it. Those who were going had to finance their own trip there. We had to memories many scriptures before we headed out so we could be prepared spiritually. Our goal was to go and help the local church that needed a lot of help on their church building.

Before taking this trip, I had a birthday to celebrate. So my Gene and I celebrated it together, for his was going to be during the time I would be gone on my mission trip. Our birthday is in the same month of May just a few days apart. We celebrated it at the American legion post 1. It was a great night. My companion's friend and wife attended as that was their first visit to the American legion. I met them at the front entrance and his good friend asked me how he could get this blond headed doll inside with out him knowing about it. Gene had made the remark that while I was gone he would get him a blonde, so his buddy came by with a life side blonde blow up doll. His friend wrapped it in a sheet and came in the back door of the American Legion and we hide it underneath our long table that we had set up. It was a special Friday night dinner and we had invited several couple to sit at our table. We all chatted and after dinner they started putting out birthday cards. Later on in the night when the music started playing his friend Ray walked over to the table where the doll was hidden and came out with it in front of a big crowd and said, "We didn't want you to be lonesome while Flora was gone so we got you a blonde". Everyone laughed it was such a great time.

When leaving the legion Gene danced with the blond all the way out the front door. I hated to leave my companion behind all alone. So I called his daughter in North Dakota and asked her to stay with him while I was gone. His son and his wife came down for his birthday too. On Sunday they went to church with their dad and after coming home Gene changed into casual clothes and told his son and daughter they were going to take a little drive. His daughter asked where they were going and he said, "You will know when we get there". When arriving at a small airport she said, "What are we doing here"? He said, "I'm going to jump out of that air plane and go skydiving". She said, "Are you crazy"! He told them he had always wanted to do it and today was the day. He knew if he didn't do it while I was away in the Bahamas he wouldn't be able to do it at all.

A lot was done before we took off on our mission trip from memory work to drills before leaving Titusville Florida. One of our drills was to stand on plats. One board would connect one plat to another. Every member, all twelve of us were to stand on these and cross over one boar to another. The purpose to this was to teach us to depend on each other and to deal with each other in such tight and close proximity and to teach us problem solving too.

We were allowed a certain number of pounds on the plain we were taking; this included our selves, suitcases and supply. When the trailer was loaded at the church we looked like hill Billies, we had our picture taken while sitting on our supply and standing by the loaded trailer. After arriving at the airport we all helped load our missionary plane and behold when they weighed us, we were five hundred pounds over the limit so the pilot had to go get another plane. We then had to unload what we had loaded into to the first plane and reload it all into the new one. In the mean time while our pilot was getting our other plane to load we sat under the wings of our first plane and ate our sack lunches. Once everything was loaded and we were settled in out seats our pilot gave us all the emergency instructions as to what to do in case we landed in the water and before take off our pilot had a word of prayer with us for a safe trip.

When we arrived at the customs the minister from the church there in the Bahamas that we were going to help was there waiting for us with an old yellow school bus. We then had to transfer all our supply again from the plain to the old yellow bus. After all our things and supply were loaded, we realized there was no room for us. So we had to sit on top of our supply, some of us on the floor, we all got on, but we sure did have a load. Once we were on the bus, I sat right behind the driver and I was shock to see him put a pair of scissors into the ignition to start it. I couldn't believe my eyes, we all laughed about this. I was hoping our bus would just make it to the little town of Nicole. Our goal on this trip was to build church benches, replace the doors and commodes. At the end we ended up building seventeen benches. These were all built at the church so we could have electricity. Some of the girls and boys sanded the benches after they were put together, then it was passed down like an assembly line. They were wiped down before we could put varnish on them. When they were dried we then added a layer of lacquer on all the benches. The doors were also made the same way and process. Other workers were putting in the commodes. We had no running water or air conditioning where we were working. We carried our own drinking water and vacation bible school supply. We carried our own food this included, sandwich meats, dried cereal, crackers, cookies and other foods. After working hard all day at the church we were to meet at the school at four for vacation bible school. When we left the old house were we were allowed to stay we had to carry clean clothes with us and change at the church for vacation bible school. The ladies all had bathing suits but me and they would go to the ocean and wash up so when they would go back to the church they would feel refreshed and somewhat clean. We had different age classes for the children to attend. They would stay after school to participate in the vacation bible school. After vacation bible school their minister invited us to dinner each night at a little shack and they would serve our food out of a little square window. We sat out in the open air on wooden benches and tables, plus cats, dogs, flies and mosquitoes. Each of us had separate classrooms to give our lessons. We were all assigned things do in the house we stayed at, before we would leave in the morning. I was assigned to make coffee every morning, for they knew I was an early riser. The mosquitoes were honestly so bad that not anyone slept well that first night. There were also a number of people that slept in tents outside of the house. As I was the oldest one on this trip I had a cot to sleep on, but three others slept on a mattress on the floor. Before leaving the run down home we were staying in, we had prayer to start our day. So the following day there was items purchase to keep the mosquitoes away or at least some what under control. We had to use bed sheets to put over the window so we could dress and undress for the windows were bare. After our early morning and prayer the vacation bible school supply was loaded back onto the old yellow bus and work was about to begin all over again. We carried a big ice chest with our food too, so we could eat at the church. We would take a thirty minute break for lunch and get back to sanding and varnishing.

One of our lady members from our church put together a beautiful stain glass window for us to put in the church. This was a great experience for me, some of the other had been to the Bahamas the year before but this was my first time in the Bahamas and my first mission trip. Some of the younger ones were afraid I wouldn't hold up thru this trip and handle all the hard work. But to their surprise they had to beg me to stop and eat lunch. I have never been afraid of hard work as I was raised on a farm and brought up in a big family and was taught hard work at ah early age. The younger group was used to seeing me dressed up at church in high heals and of coarse some of them didn't now that I knew what hard work was.

After our first week of work had ended the minister there invited us to his home to a nice dinner. It was very delicious. They were very hospitable. On Sunday at the close of the week we had our final church meeting and held a Sunday night service after all the benches were set and done and put in place. We were surprised to find out that the gentleman who played their piano at the church was completely blind. He played so beautifully. They were very happy and thankful for what we had done. After vacation bible school we gave the children treats. Some did well in vacation bible school and some did not. It was a big challenge for all of us.

Our minister that went with us suggested that we have a day of relaxation. We went to a watering hole that was so nice and big. In order to get out of it you needed to pull yourself out by holding on to a rope. We all enjoyed this time together. We went back to the old house and had to clean it up. We took out the trash and burned it and picked up our mess. We all packed our suit cases to leave the next morning. Those that were in charge of the food were in charge of getting all our food supply together to head back home.

I was up very early the next morning to make coffee for everyone. After breakfast the pastor asked us to all assemble in the living room on a very long table. We did not know what our pastor was going to do. He asked each one of us to express our feelings of what had been accomplished and enjoyed. He then brought out a pan of water and said we were going to have a foot washing. (John 13:14) He started out by washing the persons feet who was closes to him. As I didn't know what the pastor had plan I had to leave and go take my support hoses off. They all had a laugh. So as the services continued it was very solitary and touched hearts. It was so touching to go through this. As I love to write I wrote a story about the church bus and named it The Old Yellow Donkey. We packed up everything back on the bus to leave and this time we didn't have to ride on top of lumber or supplies. I kept my writing pad with me almost all of the time. Shortly after we left the old house the old yellow donkey was crying for water. The driver got out our drinking water and put it in the old yellow donkey until we could get to the nearest service station. After we gave the old yellow donkey a drink, he got a nail in its hoof. So we had to patch it up and make our trip to the minister's home. He then followed us with help to drive the bus back. Going to the airport in the bus we went thru customs again and had to load all our things back on the plane. I really enjoyed my mission work and the people we met while we were there. The children and adults alike enjoyed and appreciated all that was dome for them.

Settleing down on the plane we were ready for our fly home. Different people met us at the airport to pick us up and drove us back to the First Christian Church of Titusville. Once I arrived I called Gene and had him come and pick me up. He was happy to see me and shed some tears of joy when he saw me. He had missed me. When we arrived home Gene had a welcome sign for me and helped me unload the suitcases. As we walked in the house he said for me to sit and rest and he played a DVD for me. He said he had something to show me. Shortly after it started playing it showed him skydiving. I said, "Oh no you didn't"! And he said, "oh yes I did". He laughed at my response and reaction once I realized what he had done while I was gone. His daughter and son had witnessed and taken pictures of the whole thing. By the time I got back his children had already gone back home.

I then was beginning to have eye trouble, I started going to the doctors. After a few visits to my eye doctor I was told I was developing macrodegenarative disease. This is an eye condition where u start to loose you eye sight gradually, to the point where you can no longer see. The news was shocking to me he also added that I had cataracts in both eyes too. I was told by the doctor that I would be able to see clearer once I had the cataracts surgery in both eyes. So I went ahead and had the surgery, when it was all done with, the surgery made no difference in my eye sight. It didn't make a difference at all. In fact after the surgery my eyesight got worse. I thought that maybe if I gave my eyes time to heal it would get better, but that was not the case.

We drove back home feeling very down about the outcome of the surgery. We were very hopeful that this would work. I gradually started loosing more and more of my eye sight, to the point where I can no longer sew, read, or drive. This has hit me very hard, now that I can no longer type my own work I depend on help from friends.

During this time period I felt very down, for I was use to helping other, and now I was not able to do so. I was no longer able to pick up a book and enjoy a great story, or write my own and be able to read my own work. I have written many books but, now I can't read what I have written and I have my friend Ezzy who lives across the street from me, help me get my books done. She helps take care of my medications and fills my pills for me, since I can not read the labels and know what to take. She is not just a neighbor or a helper she is my best friend. There has been so much that has happen. The bright side of this is that I have made a great friend.

During this time my companion Gene came to know the Lord. This then turn to be another bright side of darkness. After continuing to go to church and accepting him as his Lord and savior he made the choice to be baptized. To our surprise we had the baptismal services held in one of the church member's home in their swimming pool. The reason for this was there had been an accident with the churches baptismal pool and it had overflowed and done some substantial damage to the property. I took pictures of his baptism. I was so happy and proud of him for making this choice. We sent his family pictures of him being baptized.

We enjoyed going to our church together. I was called upon to help with the Lords supper trays. It was very tedious work filling the cups that represents his blood, as I was gradually loosing my eye sight at the time. It was a very good feeling doing something for the Lord. The lady that helped me had a hard time seeing also. It took us a long time to get each tray done. This was the first time and last time to fill the trays for the Lords supper. I have lost eye sight so much now that I can no longer see the words to the songs as we sing at church. The songs I know I can sing with out needing the words. I told our minister that I couldn't see the songs anymore and he said as long as you make a joyful noise to the Lord you are fine, so this I do.

I then began having trouble walking. My right knee was giving me much grief. I went to see an orthopedic and was recommending having a full knee replacement. The pain was so bad I didn't hesitate on the decision. I was ready for it. My orthopedic doctor did a wonderful job with the surgery the rehabilitation process was a different story. I was in the hospital for a few days and was then sent to a rehab center to help me recuperate and before I was allowed to come home. All of this might not sound like a Brightside of darkness after all the surgeries, but to me it is the Brightside, because a lot of pain was being relieved.

I depend deeply on the Lord and I have faith in him.

One afternoon I told my companion Gene I was going to check my blood pressure. My pulse was in the forties. I ignored it until the next morning because I had a doctors' appointment at nine am the next day. When I walked into the doctors office and he checked my pulse he said I needed to go to the hospital immediately. I was checked in right away and I was told I would need a pace maker. We started all the preparations to have my pace maker put in.

Time goes by so slow because I can not write fast enough I love fiction and I feel safe and great among my characters. I know I am getting up in age but I have not lost my feeling for writing. I have been slowed down with the pace maker, congestive heart failure, and stents in my heart. I was in the hospital seven days with blood thinning treatments, for I was developing blood clots. I was put on many medications; the doctors have had a hard time keeping all my levels regulated. But at this time it seems like we have it under control. I don't look on the dark side of life or I would be too unhappy with myself and others. I have been told by my companion Gene I see things thru rose color glasses. I would rather see the light of life rather than darkness. I use the serenity prayer a lot in my life it is the most important thing to remember.

Gene soon learned that I was writer and a poet. He read much of my material. He said that I should get my work published. So now I'm having my books printed. It has been a challenge for me at age eighty three. I hope to get many more published and realize what I have dreamed for, for many years.

As time goes on memory lingers in my heart. My walls are lined with pictures of my children and grandchildren. This is for my family to have some of my memories to read.

*T*o all the young people out there, I hope some of this message gets through especially to young pregnant girl know that abortion is not a solution.

www.ingramcontent.com/pod-product-compliance
Lightning Source LLC
Chambersburg PA
CBHW020404290526
45785CB00005B/2434